I Love My Pet
FISH

Aaron Carr

MEDIA ENHANCED BOOKS
AV2 BY WEIGL™
ADDED VALUE • AUDIO VISUAL

www.av2books.com

AV² provides enriched content that supplements and complements this book. Weigl's AV² books strive to create inspired learning and engage young minds in a total learning experience.

Your AV² Media Enhanced books come alive with...

Audio
Listen to sections of the book read aloud.

Video
Watch informative video clips.

Embedded Weblinks
Gain additional information for research.

Try This!
Complete activities and hands-on experiments.

Key Words
Study vocabulary, and complete a matching word activity.

Quizzes
Test your knowledge.

Slide Show
View images and captions, and prepare a presentation.

... and much, much more!

Go to **www.av2books.com**, and enter this book's unique code.

BOOK CODE

N925228

AV² by Weigl brings you media enhanced books that support active learning.

Published by AV² by Weigl
350 5th Avenue, 59th Floor New York, NY 10118
Website: www.av2books.com www.weigl.com

Library of Congress Cataloging-in-Publication Data
Carr, Aaron.
-Fish / Aaron Carr.
   p. cm. -- (I love my pet)
ISBN 978-1-61690-922-2 (hardcover : alk. paper) -- ISBN 978-1-61913-021-0 (pbk) -- ISBN 978-1-61690-568-2 (online)
1. Goldfish--Juvenile literature. I. Title.
SF458.G6C37 2012
639.3'7484--dc23
                    2011025201

Printed in the United States of America in North Mankato, Minnesota
3 4 5 6 7 8 9 0 17 16 15 14 13

032013
WEP280313

Project Coordinator: Aaron Carr   Art Director: Terry Paulhus
Weigl acknowledges Getty Images, iStock, and Dreamstime as image suppliers for this title.

I Love My Pet

FISH

CONTENTS

4

I love my pet fish.
I take good care of her.

5

My pet fish was a fry.
She was very small.

Newborn goldfish
are smaller than an eyelash.

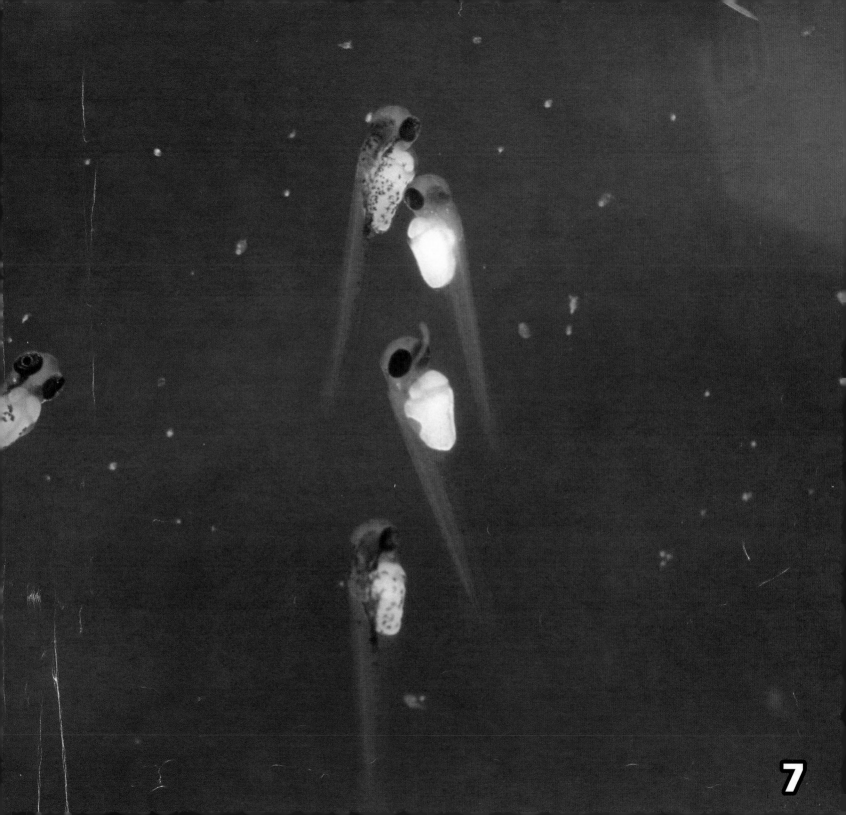

7

8

My pet fish
will grow to be large.
I have to get her
a big tank.

9

10

My pet fish can change colors.
Her color changes
to match the things around her.

Too much light
may turn goldfish white.

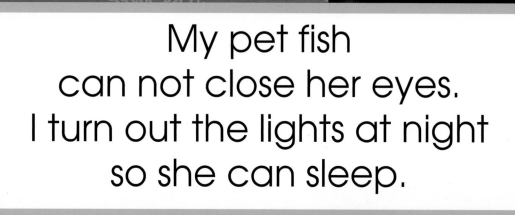

My pet fish
can not close her eyes.
I turn out the lights at night
so she can sleep.

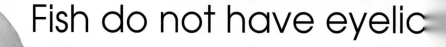

Fish do not have eyelic

My pet fish
moves when she sleeps.
I try not to wake her.

15

My pet fish
only eats once a day.
I feed her at the same time
each day.

My pet fish
needs clean water every week.
It is my job to clean her fish tank.

I help make sure
my pet fish is healthy.
I love my pet fish.

FISH FACTS

This page provides more detail about the interesting facts found in the book. Simply look for the corresponding page number to match the fact.

Pages 4-5

I love my pet fish. I take good care of her. Fish come in many sizes, shapes, and colors. Fish are beautiful pets, but they need regular care. The water in a fish tank must be monitored closely to keep your fish safe and healthy. Fish owners must learn to recognize fish behavior patterns and signs of distress to ensure their fish stay healthy.

Pages 6–7

My pet fish was a fry. He was very small. Baby fish are called fry. Most newborn fry are about 0.25 inches (1.3 centimeters) long. Fry are born in groups of up to 250. For the first few weeks, fry should be kept away from bigger fish. Large fish often eat small fries. Raising fry requires much care and should be left to experienced fish owners.

Pages 8–9

My pet fish will grow to be large. I had to get her a big tank. Most fish mature in one year, but they continue to grow throughout their lives. Fish need about 30 square inches (194 sq. cm) of water for every inch (2.5 cm) of fish. Two goldfish that are 3 inches (7.6 cm) long need about 180 square inches (1,161 sq. cm) of aquarium space.

Pages 10–11

My pet fish can not close her eyes. I turn out the lights at night so he can sleep. Fish do not have eyelids. This means that fish cannot close their eyes. In order to maintain a regular sleep cycle, fish owners must make sure to turn out the lights in both the aquarium and the room the aquarium is in during the night.

Pages 12–13

My pet fish can change colors. Her color changes to match the things around her. Some fish can change color to blend in with their environment. This helps them hide from other animals. Goldfish change color based on light. Low light produces a gold color, while too much light may result in a white goldfish.

Pages 14–15

My pet fish moves when he sleeps. I try not to wake her. Fish do not sleep the same way that humans do. Most fish move while sleeping. This is to maintain their balance and position in the water. Other fish rest on the bottom of their tank or in plants. It is important not to startle your fish while it is sleeping.

Pages 16–17

My pet fish only eats once a day. I feed her at the same time each day. Most fish only need to eat once or twice each day. Different types of fish have different diet needs. Talk to a veterinarian to determine the proper diet for your fish. Be sure not to overfeed your fish. Overfeeding can make her sick.

Pages 18–19

My pet fish needs clean water every week. It is my job to clean her fish tank. Fish tanks should be cleaned about once a week. Changes in water conditions can cause stress and illness in fish. Only replace one-quarter to one-third of the water in the tank at one time. Place your fish in a temporary tank during cleaning.

Pages 20–21

I help my pet fish stay healthy. I love my pet fish. Check your fish often for signs of illness. If you notice changes in eating, sleeping, or activity patterns, your fish may be sick. Changes in the color or condition of gills and fins may also be warnings of illness. If you notice these signs, contact a veterinarian for advice right away.

WORD LIST

Research has shown that as much as 65 percent of all written material published in English is made up of 300 words. These 300 words cannot be taught using pictures or learned by sounding them out. They must be recognized by sight. This book contains 57 common sight words to help young readers improve their reading fluency and comprehension. This book also teaches young readers several important content words, such as proper nouns. These words are paired with pictures to aid in learning and improve understanding.

Page	Sight Words First Appearance
4	good, her, I, my, of, take
6	a, an, are, she, small, than, very, was
9	be, big, get, grow, have, large, to, will
11	around, can, change, light, may, much, the, things, too, turn, white
12	at, close, eyes, night, not, out, so
15	moves, try, when
17	day, each, eats, once, only, same, time
18	every, is, it, needs, water
21	help, make

Page	Content Words First Appearance
4	fish
6	eyelash, fry, goldfish
9	tank
11	light
12	eyelids
17	time

Check out av2books.com for activities, videos, audio clips, and more!

1 Go to av2books.com

2 Enter book code   N 9 2 5 2 2 8

3 Fuel your imagination online!

www.av2books.com